100 Reflections on Life and Riding

SNOWBOARD
WISDOM

Nick Appl

Cover illustration: Dan Seward

Illustrations: Dan Seward

Dedication

For all my families; the snow-loving thrill seekers, the psychologically curious, the unconventional, the peaceful and the rowdy, and especially those closest through blood and marriage. I couldn't have done it without you.

Contents

Introduction

The inspiration to write this book came to me while studying psychology. I was 29 years old, a new father, and coming to terms with the dramatic changes that were occurring in my life. As I sat through countless lectures on psychological theories of human behavior and thought I found myself relating them to situations and experiences I'd had while snowboarding. It didn't necessarily change any of the concepts, but it did make them more interesting and I was more engaged. The seed was planted.

I went straight to the mental health front lines after graduating with a job at a residential treatment center for adolescent boys with behavioral problems. Many had come from the most nightmarish home situations imaginable. Understandably, they were not pleased to be there and arrived with a deep distrust of adults. It was our job as "mental health experts" to somehow get these boys motivated and engaged in the therapeutic process. That's a tall order for trusting and stable teenagers (unicorns?), let alone kids whose case files read like horror stories. But like any profession, psychology has some effective tools for even the most difficult cases.

This particular facility utilized a lot of outdoor

activities as part of individualized treatment plans. We would go on an adventure and then use that experience as a catalyst for processing thoughts, feelings, and behaviors. Hopefully, with repetition and reflection the dysfunctional habits would be replaced with appropriate behaviors and skills. Despite the frequent disappointments, insults, and total disregard for the process, we did witness some remarkable turnarounds. As a result, my idea for a book about snowboarding as a tool for self-discovery was beginning to grow.

I started leading group discussions that used activities like snowboarding as analogies for everyday life and my suspicions about self-awareness were confirmed. These kids were much more comfortable viewing themselves and their world through the lens of something they were already familiar with or passionate about. The appropriateness of behaviors was easier to understand and acknowledge with this indirect approach. And most importantly, they began to realize their power to create the changes they desired. My idea was blossoming and I knew I had to write this book.

The first version was shot down by every publisher I sent a proposal to. No shocker since I'd never been published, have no name recognition, and the topic of snowboarding seemed to be completely off the publishing radar. Life went on, I kept tinkering with the manuscript, getting rejection letters, and eventually reached my point of burn-out on the front lines of the mental health battlefield. Like a resilient plant, or maybe a weed, the book idea persisted.

This book is the culmination of my 20 years riding a snowboard and 10 years of daydreaming about snowboarding in relation to human psychology. I consider the finished product to be a tool for self-discovery and a catalyst for reflection. As such, deciding when and how to use any of the material will depend on the reader's objective. I can suggest that it is intended for building healthy relationships, developing values, gaining self-awareness, and otherwise growing and evolving as a person, but it's really up to you. The 100 entries are a nod to the pursuit of getting 100 riding days in a season. Whether you read one per day or all in one sitting, my wish is that you'll learn something about yourself or the world that brings you joy, peace, or understanding. Happy reading and riding!

Independent Thought

Thinking independently requires an active awareness of the influences we encounter on a daily basis. TV, internet, friends, advertising, culture, family and countless other persuasive forces creep into our brains and make an impact. This inflow is constant and persistent, taking advantage of our brains' instinct to absorb information. Luckily, there are habits we can develop to limit the influences: avoiding the worst sources, recognizing manipulation as it occurs, and processing the effects of external dynamics. Independent thought gave birth to snowboarding and fuels its progression. We can use it to create the life we want as well.

1.

Freshies

Fresh tracks and their uplifting sense of freedom do not come by copying anyone else. If you want to leave your unique mark in any setting, have the courage to believe in yourself and your vision of how something should be done, and then, rip it!

2.

Know Your Passion

Aware of it or not, everyone has a passion. Many people enjoy snowboarding and will go if given the opportunity. For others snowboarding is a passion and substantial influence in the lifestyle they create; a source of deep satisfaction. It's important to recognize where our passions exist because they often don't make sense and get little support from others. Following a passion with peace of mind requires independent thought and openness to intuition. Find it and follow it; your happiness is at stake.

3.

Shiny Objects

What's a good strategy to resist clever marketing campaigns and wasteful consumption? If a product facilitates true happiness like more opportunities to snowboard, get some! Splitboards have made riding powder and experiencing the backcountry accessible and appealing to more people. Softer flex, rockered boards make learning to ride easier and allow "mature" snowboarders more sliding pleasure. On the flip side, products come out every year with tons of hype but unable to deliver anything of substance. Spending wisely equals more fun and less work.

4.

Philosophy of Life

As each snowboarding season passes we develop our style, priorities, and a perspective on the experience. Together they become a personal philosophy on snowboarding. The truer we stay to our snowboarding philosophy the more satisfaction we get from riding. Sounds simple, but when the influences and distractions start leading us away from that personal vision it gets more difficult. Such is life and in order to live in a manner that is true to a personal philosophy of life, a conscious effort and independent thought are necessary.

Freedom

If there's a universal feeling or reward common to the entire spectrum of snowboarding experiences, it is freedom. We feel it in an unmistakably profound way. Some would say it is the core value of their snowboarding passion. It is vital to snowboard culture. Similarly, it is an essential element to a satisfying life: the key to feeling alive. Reflecting on the freedom felt while snowboarding should provide ample direction to finding it elsewhere.

5.

Choices

Snowboarding choices like where, how, and with whom we ride contribute to the pronounced sense of freedom that gets us stoked on riding. Epic terrain and conditions may provide the best options, but as it is with circumstances in life, ideal situations are limited. No worries. As long as choices exist you are free to create your reality.

Effort & Sacrifice

If you want to experience freedom on a snow-board, you have to earn it. Paying that price includes all of the effort and sacrifice that went into creating the opportunity to ride a line that sets you free. This formula can be applied to any pursuit in life. Yep, freedom isn't free.

7.

Hater Shackles

A wise guy (or gal) once said, "Those who anger you control you." Imagine taking a run where your focus is on all that annoys or angers you. People and tracks everywhere, not enough of this, too much of that, blah, blah blah. It doesn't have to get you rattled. Adjusting expectations, getting creative, or making a conscious decision to stay positive is often all it takes to regain your sense of freedom when the hater shackles come out. Don't put 'em on anywhere or any-time; they're ugly and restrictive.

8.

Creative Expression

Find some liberation with a little creation. Snowboarding is a super-duper outlet for creative thought and action, hence the feelings of freedom. When you are free, you create and when you create, you are free. Keep this in mind anytime life starts feeling restrictive.

Stoke

The literal definition of stoke refers to increasing the heat of a fire by stirring the embers. It's also a fitting description of the powerful jolt from a riding session. The inner fire that propels us through life is stirred, at times to the same degree as a raging bonfire. This can also become a reference point to gauge how we are living our lives. Without that fire we become cold, sluggish, and uninspired. When it's burning we feel powerful and alive. To lead an inspired life it is very important to learn multiple ways to stoke that inner fire in the same way snowboarding does.

9.

Real Reality

An important lesson from getting stoked on a board is that it is the result of doing something real, in a real environment, with real consequences. It is not virtual, superficial, or contrived. Life in general is more likely to get you stoked if you pursue a reality with the truth and consequences of riding your snowboard. Live real, be real, stay stoked.

10.

Going All In

Think about the best day(s) you ever had snowboarding. Did you hesitate, withdraw, or give a partial effort? Most likely you were all in with your focus and energy and it contributed to getting you stoked as much as the conditions, friends, and location of those epic days. Perfect scenarios make going all in very easy. But they are the exception and the challenges we typically face make total commitment more daunting. What snowboarding teaches in this regard is that if you believe in what you are doing, go for it all the way if you want to be stoked. It's proof that what you put into something determines what you get out of it.

11.

Mind Body Soul

Snowboarding involves creative expression (mind), athleticism (body) and a meaningful connection with environment (soul). All three have the power to stoke you out in their own way. No wonder snowboarding feels so good. Separately or all at once, keep finding ways to engage the mind, body and soul.

12.

Inner Fire

Determination, passion, will power, ambition, and energy exemplify the inner fire propelling you through life. No wonder it feels like anything is possible when the stoke is high; your fire is roaring. What will you do with it? Find a more meaningful use than dousing it après. Unless there's a good band. Or good company. Or you have nothing important to contribute and no need to conserve a little. Anyway, respect and appreciate the power.

Consequences

Consequences, often confused with punishment, can also be positive. They happen because of, or result from, something prior. Sometimes immediate, like pain from wipeouts or the stoke of a powder day, sometimes eventual, like gaining skills or wisdom, consequences will always be related to the choices we make. Snowboarding is ripe with examples and teaches us how to benefit from honestly evaluating positive or negative consequences of our actions. To do otherwise is to live in denial.

13.

Reality Check

Even on days with perfect, forgiving snow, a tree or rock will be just as hard and capable of dishing out pain to snap you back into reality. This is important to remember because when everything is going well or going off, people tend to let their guard down. Who wants to let caution ruin a moment? Someone who doesn't want an epic moment to become a long episode of pain, that's who. Know the risks, and then proceed. And by all means, let it rip! Fear not riders, in snowboarding and in life, reality checks can be minimized by awareness of consequences.

14.

Risk vs. Reward

Despite the plethora of risk, the rewards, those sweet, sweet rewards make riding a snowboard a worthwhile pursuit. Very rarely in life or snowboarding is it possible to eliminate risk. Therefore, we must learn how to evaluate risk versus reward instead of denying the risk is there or giving it too much power. It seems that successful people develop habits to acknowledge risk without freezing in fear or acting recklessly. It's a balancing act. Snowboarding provides experiences with fear, ignorance, and successful resolution of encountering risks. Don't forget what each feels like.

15.

Responsibility

Accidents, wipe-outs, and blown opportunities happen for all sorts of reasons. When they do, you have a choice either to take responsibility or point the finger and blame. Sure there was ice, fog, flat light, bad take-offs and transitions, distractions, and people working against you. But if you blame them, you give up your power to them too. Instead focus on your role and what YOU could have done differently. That's the path to learning, growing, and overcoming the challenges of snowboarding and everyday life.

16.

Limitations

Snowboarding is perfectly suited to teach us about recognizing limits and what it takes to expand them. This serves two purposes; it can spare you unnecessary pain and reveal where to focus on improving. If you didn't catch your edges while learning to ride, you would be more likely to go too fast and really get hurt. The pain and embarrassment of slamming also forces you to concentrate on proper technique. This holds true for all levels of skill. Some people will always be driven to push the limits while others find and accept them. Awareness of personal limits is another form of self-knowledge, without which you are highly limited.

Boundaries

Boundaries are similar to limitations. They can be physical or mental, man-made or existing in nature. One thing they are not however, is avoidable. Motivation to progress on a snowboard will inevitably lead to testing these boundaries and our ability to grow as individuals. We all develop a method and a style for doing this which then becomes a habit. Sometimes these habits are tools that help us achieve goals and sometimes they become roadblocks to success. The point is we need to be aware of how we approach and deal with boundaries. Your relationship with boundaries in snowboarding applies to life in general.

17.

Authority

Authority figures, as well as their rules, can present a complicated and frustrating form of boundaries. Our approach and attitude here is the key to satisfactory outcomes. With ski patrol or resort boundaries, recognize that they have important jobs and protect many people from pain and suffering. If they cramp your style and become too restrictive, move on, like into the backcountry or to a more permissive locale. It seems that the happiest people, including snowboarders, either understand and accept boundaries or find the space they desire elsewhere. If you must, fight them as a last resort.

18.

Physical Limits

Physical limitations change with fitness, age, and circumstances. If you want to keep operating at a high level you have to stay tuned into the body's messages. Snowboarding is great at teaching when to push on, when to back off, and the consequences of not paying attention. Developing this awareness with riding prepares you to make good decisions and be less restricted in general.

19.

Mental Blocks

Mental boundaries can be very sneaky. Once established, they disguise themselves with excuses and will often highjack emotions to undermine goals and responsibilities. And then one day, by force of will, a friend's urging, or a surge of inspiration, you decide to challenge the self-imposed boundary. Landing a new trick, riding the line you eyed forever, or maybe moving to a dream location are potential rewards for such bravery. Developing a strategy in snowboarding to prevent boundaries from becoming strict limitations and stagnation is a valuable skill for living well.

20.

Progression
(patiently)

Pushing the limits and personally progressing are invaluable to the snowboarding experience, a source of great pride and satisfaction. The trick is to stay patient with the process. Many a new season ends prematurely because someone thinks they are in late-season form. Put the work in before going for the big payday; this isn't the lottery.

Ride-About

A ride-about is similar to the Australian practice of a walkabout. During a walkabout someone takes a break from work to focus on other matters; like a long vacation or sabbatical. Ride-about is taking a leave from career development and material acquisition to whole-heartedly pursue snowboarding. This may result in clarifying career-type goals, but the priority is snowboarding; anything else is a bonus. Ride-abouts can last one winter or span several years, it's different for everyone. The purpose is detachment from society's pressure to fill a certain role or meet expectations in order to define personal priorities. It is a luxury. It can also be a springboard to meaningful, productive achievements.

21.

(Mainstream) Values/Career

A key element to a ride-about is the temporary suspension of career-oriented goals. Allow yourself a break from mainstream pressures and go for maximum fun and adventure. If you learn about yourself and develop your own values during this time, you'll make better choices and have more to offer when you are ready for a career.

22.

Minimize

Most people learn to get by with less while on a ride-about. This experience alone can change the trajectory of someone's life.

23.

Identity

When you start snowboarding the first goal is to learn how to turn the board. After that, your snowboarding identity begins to develop in line with the type of riding that speaks to you. Whatever route you choose should come from the heart. If you learn this trick in snowboarding you can do it anywhere.

24.

Friends

The friendships formed during a ride-about are often the most valuable part. Snowboarding is truly a melting pot and chances are you will meet people you never would have met without it. Appreciate your path, the people you meet along the way and the need for community and connection in general.

Temporary Selfishness

While it's true that a lot of selfishness is negative, there are also many ways that selfishness is both positive and necessary. Taking care of oneself and focusing on personal growth are selfish; but they also allow people to become independent and effective. As responsibilities change and become larger in life, the selfish work a person has done becomes more valuable. Snowboarding is primarily a selfish act which we do for personal enjoyment, but it can also empower generosity. The process involves accumulating skills, values, and experience (selfish) that can be passed on to the benefit of others (unselfish). Turning selfishness into selflessness is worthy of any bag of tricks.

25.

Preparation

If anyone tells you that snowboarding is selfish, agree with them. Also let them know you will have more to contribute in selfless endeavors because you spent time getting to know yourself through snowboarding. Don't just be good, be good for something.

26.

Defining Values

Values will guide a person through confusing and stressful times. They also influence decisions, big or small, that steer our trajectories through life. Snowboarding values lead to support of certain companies and causes, not because it's easy or convenient, but because they are consistent with our values for the present and future state of snowboarding. Values make hard work and difficult choices feel good as selfish pleasures with a greater purpose.

27.

Growth

Get healthy, make friends, challenge yourself, scare yourself, and keep exploring as a means to individual growth. Snowboarding is fertile ground in this regard. As we reflect on riding experiences we harvest what has grown within. The change is real and with an awareness of personal transformation within ourselves there's reason to have faith in change and growth beyond ourselves. A person or cause could probably use your help right now.

28.

Success

Knowing how to succeed is a skill. Learning to turn, negotiating a double black diamond, landing a trick, and going to new places are examples of snowboarding success. Think about a success you've had riding. How did you handle opportunities to quit? Were there influences or feedback from others? How did you overcome fears and distractions? Your answers can manifest success anywhere.

Adventure & Discovery

Adventure and discovery are integral to snowboarding and living a full life. Adventures are exciting; discoveries are rewarding. It takes initiative and persistence to generate a satisfying experience, particularly when something unexpected happens. In snowboarding, surprises are typically accepted as part of the deal. As such, we are better prepared to cope with them and use them to our advantage. With intention and practice an open, flexible outlook develops. Challenge yourself to employ this mentality beyond riding and see what else you can overcome.

29.

Open-mindedness

If you've ever had to employ new tactics in response to poor weather, sketchy snow conditions, or an unexpected obstacle while riding, you've probably felt your mind stretch a bit. A simple shift in attitude, perspective, or approach can be difficult when frustrations build but they often hold the key to success. Just like your body, your mind excels when nimble and limber.

30.

Self-knowledge
(Inner Terrain)

Your thoughts and behaviors carrying you through the world resemble your skills on a snowboard. Similar to progression in snowboarding you need patience, strength, guidance, courage, focus, and persistence to gain self-knowledge. And maybe a book or two. If you're up for it, what you find and experience might get you just as stoked as your adventures on a board.

31.

Curiosity

The dictionary defines curiosity as, "the desire to learn or know about anything." It's typical that when you practice curiosity while snowboarding, the experience is richer and the stoke higher. Discovering new lines, stashes, zones, styles, and friends often start with the thought, "I wonder if". It's a mental shift that opens the door to possibilities. Stay curious my friends.

32.

Surprises

If you can turn snowboarding surprises into fun adventures, you have the ability and perspective to do the same when life throws you a curveball. All it takes is an open mind and a willing attitude. Anyway, it's really not an adventure until the plan gets blown up.

Humans & Nature

Getting along with the natural world requires acceptance of forces beyond our control and enduring poor conditions with patience. Snowboarding will give you plenty of practice with both. On one hand, snowboarding ingeniously harnesses gravity and seasonal elements to create thrilling moments of pure joy. On the other, it subjects us to the painful possibilities of gravity and stubbornly withholds the conditions we desire. Most of the time nature requires us to accept conditions, adapt plans, and adjust expectations according to what is available. Our options to fight this reality may be very limited, but our creativity, openness, and determination can be strengthened.

33.

Acceptance

Snowboarding is all about the snow. Typically, the more the better. We plot and scheme and plan to get as much as possible. When Mother Nature doesn't cooperate, it's time to practice acceptance (unless you have an unlimited travel budget). Adapt and overcome, you never know what will happen.

34.

Seasons

Seasons demonstrate that no matter how we feel about a situation, it is not permanent. Despite your love for it, winter will end. Life has a similar ebb and flow to be aware of. Good times must end and challenging intervals are bound to occur, but you can anticipate the fluctuation as a refreshing and natural balance. Imagine the shock and dismay if spring were unexpected. Enjoy the moment, but realize it won't last.

35.

Gravity

Gravity can be viewed as a foe that holds one down and causes falls or as the ally that propels your board and makes flight special. It's both and you cannot change it. But, if you can perceive and interact with natural forces positively, your chances for success are greater than if you fight or deny them. The same relationship exists elsewhere in nature and the approach you choose will affect your experience.

36.

Nature's Indifference

As the man-made world increasingly seeks to protect people, self-responsibility gets diminished. Thankfully, the natural world has no capacity for such things. If someone dies snowboarding, nature will not pause for a second to consider making changes. Embracing this reality is the first step to making better decisions. Take responsibility for yourself and live to ride another day.

Goals

Snowboarding is a great way to learn about defining goals and decisive action. Every turn you make on a snowboard contains a goal and a purpose. You are moving in a chosen direction for a specific reason. When you decide where to go and how to get there it creates a real sense of freedom. It may be more difficult to manifest such pure freedom outside snowboarding, but it's just as necessary to be moving with purpose if you want to feel it at all. Snowboarding is full of surprises and being forced to adopt new goals on the fly keeps us stimulated and engaged. Such is life.

37.

Perseverance

The nature of snowboarding requires sustained effort to overcome obstacles and achieve goals. First-try successes are special because they are rare. The difficulty in achieving your snowboarding goals undoubtedly made it that much sweeter when you landed the trick, survived the gnarly run you eyed for years, or just strapped in after a long recovery from injury. Remember this lesson when your focus or motivation starts to fade in pursuit of any life goal. Do not be denied!

38.

Challenge Yourself

Life is full of challenges. Sometimes you choose them and sometimes they choose you. Either way, go after them with enthusiasm. When you begin snowboarding the challenges are constant and opportunities for success are plentiful. Novelty is good like that. As you progress, the challenges and satisfaction diminish unless you push yourself. Whenever you find yourself seeking a more rewarding life consider this example from snowboarding.

39.

Define, Decide, Act

If you love winter and snow you know they never seem to last long enough. As a result, snowboarding goals are often clearly defined in terms of details like timing and conditions. This is a valuable habit because nature's opportunities are fleeting and must be seized with urgency. A thoughtful approach to your goals allows you to act with decisiveness as well as spontaneity when the conditions set up just right. Chances to fulfill any goal in life can vanish as quickly as the snow so get them while you can!

40.

Bravery

Every run on a snowboard involves a large goal (the destination) along with smaller ones (route, tricks, etc.). Ready to oppose those goals are frightening obstacles and opportunities to quit; some are real, some perceived. Do you let the fear win? Courage to recognize and overcome difficulties in snowboarding mimics scenarios of everyday life. Failure might be painful, but not as much as giving up. Be brave, have fun, and do your best. If you can do that, you've succeeded.

Health

Your health is your responsibility. A simple, real-istic path to greater health is to every day move your body, manage your stress, and stimulate your mind. Snowboarding teaches the habit and value of all three. Finding more ways to accom-plish these three objectives will naturally create a lifestyle of good health and good times.

41.

Motivation

Good health is as valuable as what you do with it. Snowboarding is an outstanding source of motivation when it comes to health because it presents tangible benefits for maintaining robustness. Better health = better riding (or whatever you aspire to).

42.

Triple Play

Recipe for good health: move your body, manage your stress, and stimulate your mind. Repeat daily. This is why riding a snowboard feels so good.

43.

Prevention vs. Damage Control

Many people live in poor health, only working on it when physical or mental conditions force them to. This is damage control and similar to approaching snowboarding as something to be endured instead of the tremendously enjoyable activity that it is. Damage control will keep you alive, but preventative action like eating nutritious food, getting appropriate rest, and staying physically fit make you FEEL alive. Don't wait until you are sick or in pain to take care of yourself. Your best riding and most satisfying life require good health.

44.

Supportive Environment

People drawn to snowboarding are general-
ly active year-round. In the off-season there's
surfing, skating, hiking, fishing, hunting, biking,
climbing, and such where the mental, physical,
and spiritual needs of good health can be met.
Thus, a lifestyle is created. Communities develop around lifestyles and, like many a mountain
town, the community and the lifestyle support
one another with priorities like good health.
That support is often critical in sustaining positive habits. By choosing a healthy environment/
community, good health comes easier.

Competition

The topic of competition probably brings out the most love-hate reactions within snowboarding. What can't be denied is that it has a huge presence. Competitive snowboarding's capacity to influence and the emotions it generates make it too important to ignore. This also indicates there are many lessons snowboarding's competitive side can teach about the world and ourselves.

45.

Healthy Comparisons

An accurate perception of oneself is often the greatest reward of competing. You may be "the man" (or woman) at your local hill, but entering an event that draws riders from far and wide will impact that assessment. Whether it's confirmed or denied, your self regard now has greater perspective. The new information can motivate further dedication, inspire creativity, keep an ego in check, and generate progression. What you do with the information is up to you; just don't hide behind excuses if you don't like it.

46.

Performance Under Pressure

One undeniable aspect of competing is the demand for performance under pressure and scrutiny. You can learn a ton about managing nerves, sharpening focus, and developing body awareness by competing. These skills never lose their value.

47.

Progression vs. Winning

While it is true that most competitors enter events with the intention of winning, progression seems to be more beneficial in general. Progression in snowboarding happens both individually and collectively. As individuals push each other to improve for a podium spot, snowboarding gains in diversity of skills, advances in gear, and in the evolution of competitive formats. Winning might represent a goal or destination, but progression is the journey. As snowboarders, we should celebrate the progression-driven approach to competition because it represents self-improvement.

48.

Soulless Money

Competitions demonstrate the range of effects money has on people and culture. On one hand money is a prize incentive for progression, a means to celebrate and support worthwhile causes, and a catalyst for snowboarding evolution. At the same time it has the potential to create jealousy, dishonesty, infatuation, and abuse of the environment and resources. Many within the snowboarding community have worked hard to find a balance and healthy pursuit of money on the competitive scene. Too much focus on money results in a loss of soul. This is not exclusive to snowboarding.

Pain & Failure

To fall down while snowboarding is to fail in the sense that staying upright is ultimately the goal, unless you're in some kind of wipe-out contest. Anyway, we all fail and must also learn how to respond to it. The great lesson in snowboarding lies in the fact that we expect and also accept some degree of failure. It's the only way to avoid dwelling on mistakes. In order to improve as a snowboarder we have to recognize and take ownership of the aspects we control or influence. When we choose accountability we avoid wasting energy on blaming others or making excuses, a vicious cycle of self-defeat.

49.

Coping Skills

Laughing at yourself, accepting mistakes, own-
ing your choices, and having patience with a
process are just some of the ways to deal with
setbacks. Snowboarding isn't always easy but
neither is life. Chances are whatever method
keeps you on track to achieve a snowboarding
goal will transfer to everyday situations.

50.

Learning Process

Learning how to snowboard can be a rough process with pain endured along the way. But it's also a great opportunity to build tolerance and strength regarding an inevitability of life so a little pain doesn't keep us from reaching our goals. In the same sense, constantly avoiding any and all situations with the potential for pain leaves us weak and vulnerable to minor discomforts. Don't obsess over living a pain-free existence. We often don't realize our own strength until forced to cope with physical, mental, or emotional pain. Avoiding all pain and failure is denying a key part of the learning process and growth on a snowboard or any other pursuit will be stunted.

51.

Ownership

Taking ownership of what happens in life can be one of the most difficult and uncomfortable things to do. It is also one of the most empowering actions we can take. While not easy, it's as simple as looking at your own actions as the cause of how much you get to ride, where you are riding, who you ride with, how well you ride, and ultimately, how much fun you are having on your snowboard. Taking ownership of your snowboarding or life is acknowledging that the most powerful force in your life is you.

52.

Shifting
Blame/Excuses

No amount of blaming or excuse making ever made a person into a better snowboarder. Poor snow, flat light, wrong wax, gapers in your way, blah, blah, blah. These things happen everywhere and must be overcome. If you want to learn a skill or dial in a trick, bear down with effort and determination. Playing the blame game is giving up your power.

Respect

It seems the element of rebellion is the glue that unites snowboarding culture, keeps it exciting, and makes it more interesting in general. The importance of respect is not diminished by any of that. We still have to maintain a general regard for ourselves, others, and the resources that sustain us in order to avoid self-destruction. The Golden Rule, you reap what you sow, Karma, what goes around, comes around are all ways of expressing "give respect, get respect". Snowboarding or otherwise, sticking up for yourself, defending your values, and resisting the mainstream current can all be done respectfully.

53.

Trees

Trees = Snowboards, Shelter, Heat, OXYGEN!, Powder Stashes, Riding Features, Fog-busters, Real Syrup, Fruits and Nuts, oh my!!! You're not hugging them?

(p.s. same goes for nature in general)

54.

For Others

The standard skier/boarder responsibility code at resorts doesn't suck. It's about respect. Respect others enough to not injure them. Duh. Respect the resort enough to not jeopardize it. Duh. Respect the potential for surprises. Duh. Respect yourself enough to be informed. Duh. You aren't expected to like others, the resort, surprises, or yourself, simply respect them. Life is easier (and more fun) if you understand the difference.

55.

For Self

Snowboarding can build self-respect while teaching what it feels like and why it matters. As we progress with riding we face challenges, develop a style and identity, and become familiar with our unique talents. The result is a profound sense of pride and worthiness. It seems that once self-respect is developed people act with integrity and also realize they deserve to be treated with respect by others. We might overlook self-respect as an element of feeling stoked, but it is a large part of it and contributes to that sense of personal power.

56.

For Pioneers

If you are aware of snowboarding's history and pioneers, you know what dedication to a vision means. Through trial and error breakthroughs occurred. By challenging the status quo an industry evolved. Minds were changed from resistance to acceptance via conviction and passion. All of this happened while the mainstream said it was a fad that would eventually go away, hopefully soon. Look how much awesomeness their efforts have given us! Give it up for snowboarding's trailblazers and let their example inspire your pioneering efforts. At the very least, know the history.

Consumerism

Sometimes we buy stuff so we can do stuff. And sometimes we do stuff so we can buy stuff. Along the way we consider need vs. want, useful vs. gimmick, appropriate vs. wasteful, and durable vs. disposable. If not, shouldn't we? When it comes to snowboarding gear these questions matter because the environment that produces them is the same environment we depend on for snowboarding to be possible. Technology creates possibilities. It also creates waste. Finding a balance that corresponds to our values is an important lesson of snowboarding.

57.

Useful or Gimmick

A lot of new equipment and devices come with "technological advances" marketed as something necessary. It takes very little effort to think about why you would be better off having it. A product that matters will actually impact your snowboarding experience in a specific, definable way. The rest is just more stuff.

58.

Resource Responsible

If we trash the planet, we destroy ourselves and snowboarding. Since large companies and operations have the biggest environmental impact, they also have the greatest potential for changing wasteful, destructive behavior. Our role as consumers is to support the most responsible ones with money and participation, prompting others to get with the program. Resorts are investing in green energy, boards are being made with fewer toxins, and outerwear is getting produced with recycled material. Vote for them with your money because everyday is Earth Day. This momentum will encourage more responsible use of resources across the board.

59.

Media Technology

Many people have a love-hate relationship with the amount and nature of media that exists. Here are two reasons to drop the hate side of that equation. First, you can unplug and go snowboarding, read a book, whatever. Second, consider how many people benefit from exposure to snowboard culture. It has an impact and influences people in real ways. Witnessing a carefree, joyous act of snowboarding can leave an impression on an otherwise uninspired person. People who do ride can share and learn from each other more easily. Like a tool, it's all about how you use it. As a resource, consume it wisely.

60.

Nature Conservation

Snowboarding heavily depends on the natural world as an "arena" for the sport. You might consider it a product with which we develop personal connections. Thus, it becomes a valued commodity. Many people do not value or respect nature because they do not feel connected to it in any meaningful (recreation, food, water, etc.) way. We can affect that by helping others become more connected through snowboarding or similar activities. To the disconnected, nature is only raw materials. Those with a connection see a finished product worth protecting and conserving.

Self-Control & Discipline

Our minds have a natural urge to make sense of what they perceive in order to feel in control. This is not necessarily a bad thing. People who are at least moderately in control of their thoughts and emotions are less anxious and stressed out than those who are not. Controlling ourselves in this regard is complicated and difficult. However, if it is lacking, that natural urge for control will manifest in wanting to control other people and situations in an unhealthy manner, like control freaks. Snowboarding constantly presents situations that require self-control and this can lead to effective self-control as a strength and habit.

61.

Fear and Courage

Fear is a biological instinct for self-preservation, a warning system that primes the body and mind for danger. Snowboarding is a great way to become familiar with the signals and to develop a response strategy. Think of a snowboarding goal you really wanted but scared the hell out of you. Visualizing, breathing, pumping yourself up, reciting a mantra or prayer; whatever worked in that moment can work in any moment eliciting fear. Your body always responds to fear the same way. Courage is the ability to manage that response and to keep going

62.

Impulsivity

In the most basic sense impulsiveness means not looking before you leap. A plush, open powder field above rocks or cliffs will play on your urges to shred. A partner's guidance or some scouting ahead of time are sometimes all it takes to avoid dangerous scenarios. But it looks so good. What if someone else gets it first? People are watching and what will they think? I want it now. Experiences like these are prime opportunities to develop an awareness of impulsive tendencies and a game plan for appropriate action.

63.

Keep Moving

Ever notice how difficult it can be to stand still with both feet strapped into your board? Life resembles this characteristic of boards in the sense that idleness leaves us vulnerable to falling. Snowboards are designed and built for mobility. People seem similarly intended for creative and productive action. Keep moving, exploring, and enjoying so you don't tip over.

64.

Trust

The scary flipside to control is trust. With practice, this too can become natural and easy. Think about how tense and vigilant you were when learning to ride. Nothing could be trusted because you felt vulnerable. With persistence you learned to relax and trust your board, body, and gravity to do their thing; get you stoked. Many people remain stuck in that exhausting beginner state in life because they never learn to trust or had it violated. Keep practicing trust, even after a hard slam.

Journey

Journeys happen with the mind, body, and spirit. The ups and downs, obstacles overcome, challenges met, and transformations that occur are all souvenirs we collect on the path of snowboarding. Utilizing the lessons of a snowboarding journey can contribute to a happy ending on any life quest.

65.

Complacency

Don't let your comfort zone become your cage. A common occurrence in mountain towns is people getting complacent and becoming jaded. Everything and everyone is viewed as an annoyance unless they are having an "epic" day. This is the result of a hunger for meaningful challenge and the brain having surplus energy. If this happens with your snowboarding or elsewhere, it is a clear signal for action and change.

66.

Balance and Adaptability

Life can be unpredictable, bumpy, and harsh. Same goes for snowboarding. In order to enjoy and succeed at both we need balance and adaptability. Snowboarders maintain balance via practice, diversity of skills, and appropriate use of resources (gear). Adaptability is achieved with an open mind, flexibility, and willingness to change with situational demands. Greater balance and adaptability results in more opportunity for enjoyment and peace of mind. Same goes for life.

67.

Surrender

There will always be times along one's journey that feel chaotic and out of control. Blind ambition and tunnel vision can amplify the obstacles standing in the way of our goals. Often we are best served by backing off until the disorder subsides as a storm passing or snowpack settling. Your plans for an epic trip or season can be drastically altered by health, snow conditions, and circumstances in general. If it is more prudent to give them priority, do it, even if it feels like surrender. It is not the same as giving up. Live to ride another day and respect the chaos along the way.

68.

Exploration

True exploration happens when embracing an attitude of curiosity and maintaining an open mind. The payoff in snowboarding comes in the form of hidden powder stashes at a resort, new urban spots or unridden zones in the backcountry. It is such a rewarding part of snowboarding that is seems obvious to also be living this way. That same curiosity and openness to discovery can be applied to knowing oneself, education on important issues, and whatever else one values. You never know what some looking around will lead to.

Perspective

An accurate perception of where we are and where we're going cannot be overstated. In snowboarding we are often rewarded with panoramic views from the top of mountains. These provide a detached, big-picture perspective of the present environment. Successful snowboarding (whatever that is to you) also requires attention to the immediate, small-picture details like specific terrain features, dialed-in equipment, and personal well-being. Together, the large and small-scale perspectives inform our snowboarding decisions, provide inspiration, and determine a course of action. A balance of broad and precise views is more than a prudent snowboarding strategy; it's a clever move in general.

69.

Go Deeper

Don't judge the day until you're at least 3 runs in. It's difficult to truly know about something, like a day in the mountains, until you've spent time going beyond the surface or first impression or first run. First impressions can be skewed by preconceived notions, attitudes, and not eating breakfast. In life and snowboarding, the process of warming up, getting into a rhythm and adjusting to conditions are valuable to your perspective as well as your performance.

70.

The Big Picture

The view from on top of a mountain often stuns people into silence and inspires contemplation. No wonder since it's so different from everyday immersion in the valley of details. When you can take in the full layout of a community or the immensity of a mountain range, suddenly new information becomes available. Take advantage of such an opportunity for reflection. There's a reason so many wise people have found enlightenment in the mountains.

71.

Details

Details matter in snowboarding and life. With riding there are many small pieces of gear that, if they fail or get overlooked, can have significant consequences. Broken straps or buckles, foggy goggles, a lost lift pass, the wrong wax, or any nuts and bolts (literally and figuratively) gone missing can turn into significant buzz kills. Simply checking them before heading out or being stocked with parts and know-how is usually adequate. There will always be surprises, but you can be ready for them.

72.

Stay Open

The fun we seek on a snowboard is no different than the happiness all people are searching for in life. We are just using different means to achieve the same goal. Be open to other methods of pursuing happiness and you'll have more options at your disposal. It only takes a couple of runs with new riding partners to see different lines or fresh takes on familiar ones. If you're truly open to possibilities it can even happen with a skier. Despite the apparent diversity among people in the mountains and elsewhere, we are all very similar.

Attachments

Attachments are worthy of thought and reflection because they have the potential to restrict growth and freedom. We are naturally and constantly attracted to ideas, places, people, and objects. Over time, attachments develop, sometimes to the extent of a fusion with our identities. The trick is learning to recognize their expiration date. Some attachments will stand the test of time and many others become "dead weight", needing to be dropped for personal growth to continue, like pruning a tree. Snowboarding provides plenty of opportunities to experiment with the nature of attachments. Reduce the clutter and you won't sputter.

73.

Material Objects

It seems natural for snowboarding "stuff" to become more personally valuable as it contributes to creating epic moments. What about when you can't or don't use it anymore? Passing it on will not erase your memory. Attachment creates that strange pull to keep objects otherwise collecting dust and cluttering our lives. A board may be too difficult to part with. It also might prove more useful and give you the most satisfaction by going to someone less fortunate. Recognizing and surrendering your attachment will make the choice easier. This is good practice developing generosity, minimalism, and simplicity.

74.

People

Similar to objects becoming burdensome, relationships with people can lose their benefits and desirability. When close friends are headed in separate directions with different goals, that bond has the potential to create negativity. Just as you would not voluntarily give up snowboarding to pursue something you don't believe in, the friends who do not share your snowboarding desire or goals should not be expected to follow your path. Doing so risks resentment and total loss of friendship. Everyone's path is different. Honor old friends, make new ones, and appreciate relationships regardless of their duration.

75.

Places

Mountain towns and the mountains themselves are easy to become attached to. They frequently create "life-changing" moments and are catalysts for personal transformation. How long a beloved spot is a healthy place to be is another matter. The answer is different for each of us and knowing when to move on can be confusing. We can recognize if a snowboarding location is appropriate and healthy by the way we feel riding there, by how much it inspires creativity, or by whether or not we envision meeting our goals there. Staying for those reasons is healthy. Remaining there simply due to attachments and fear of the unknown will not serve us in reaching our potential. Attachments to any location are similar to this experience.

76.

Ideas/Attitudes

Sometimes an idea can be the most difficult "thing" to let go of. Ideas can be held privately and we often hang onto them too long, like rancid food tucked away in the refrigerator. Our minds naturally form ideas about what is important, how things should be done, and what the outcome should be. But, think of what we'd miss out on in snowboarding if only one person, place, style, product, condition, or result were acceptable. In the moment and over time we approach snowboarding with mental flexibility and non-attachment to ideas and attitudes. This keeps the stoke high. Seems like a habit worth repeating.

Self-Awareness

Self-awareness is not just knowing about ourselves, but also understanding the internal and external effects of our behaviors and attitudes. It's an irreplaceable quality in manifesting the path we desire. But it takes time. Self-awareness in snowboarding involves learning, practicing, and integrating mental and physical skills that lead to the greatest satisfaction and pleasure. We come to know the how, what, where, and with whom we want to ride and energy is used more efficiently toward getting stoked. It seems like this would apply to life in general regarding self-awareness.

77.

Attitude

Attitude is a huge responsibility because of the impact it has on a person's reality. A positive snowboarding attitude will minimize the bad and maximize the good aspects of a run. Riding with a poor attitude does the opposite, making enjoyment more difficult and creating a vicious cycle of negativity. Fear not shredders, we always have a choice with attitude. Change your attitude; change your reality.

78.

Confidence

Find a way to cultivate confidence in yourself; your success depends on it. When you step up to a line, a trick, linking your first turns, or any other snowboarding scenario, there's usually a scene playing out in your head beforehand, like a movie preview. Whether your preview ends in failure or success, it increases the odds of the real thing playing out that same way. Positive thoughts, positive results. Confidence can become a habit.

79.

Thinking Errors/Habits

Prior to any action or behavior there will be a thought or state of mind that influences how things happen. Usually it's easiest to blame a wipeout on the snow, body position, terrain, or any number of physical elements. If you haven't already, try examining what happened in your head just before you dropped in. Pay especially close attention to what preceded positive results. When repeated, mental activity becomes a habit. If you are having a problem or mistakes keep happening, whether snowboarding or doing anything else, your state of mind should be included with the factors in need of some tweaking.

80.

Authenticity

In life and snowboarding people experiment with different styles searching for what fits and feels right. Imagine what you would sacrifice by snowboarding in uninspiring places with disagreeable people. Sounds ridiculous but it happens all the time because of pressures to conform and to deny an authentic life. Whether it's snowboarding or life in general, you only need to "keep it real" with yourself. The first step is figuring out who you are. Know yourself, know peace.

Appreciation

Positive thinking habits like appreciation for places, moments or people are often created through snowboarding experiences. When we're starved for powder and it finally dumps, every turn becomes deeply satisfying. The more places we ride the more strongly we feel about the special ones. Life can separate close friends until one day a sublime reunion occurs. Experiences like these allow a sense of appreciation to develop. Then we have the ability to be more stoked on any situation. Who wouldn't appreciate that?

81.

Epic Days

Work for unforgettable moments that are brief. If you haven't been snowboarding in poor conditions, you can't fully appreciate the best conditions. Preparation allows you to enjoy it longer and more completely. Experience gives you the perspective to understand how special something is. Every day, on or off a snowboard, is an opportunity to prepare for success.

82.

Focus on Positives

Even when the snow is AWOL or the available terrain and features are not ideal, opportunities for good times exist. Enjoying the company of friends, connecting with nature, self-examination, experimenting with gear or practicing patience are all valuable. A simple shift in focus and expectations can make a huge difference. Finding positives can be more difficult than whining and complaining, but which habit will serve you better?

83.

Simplity

Keep priorities as simple as possible. Sometimes the pursuit for more, better, and newer complicates matters so much that the purpose is lost; in this case, the joy of snowboarding. If you have the ability to go out and have fun on a snowboard, don't clutter that privilege with irrelevant concerns. Go snowboard and reap the benefits.

84.

The Dark Side

Learn to appreciate the difficult, confusing, and dark emotions for what they contribute in strength and depth of character. Snowboarding is often utilized as an outlet and processor of anger, pain, or negativity. As such, a potentially destructive force becomes motivation for creativity and soul-satisfying action. We don't have to be victims of dark emotions. They can be used as fuel to create the change we desire. If we can snowboard our way out of a funk, we must be capable of finding other ways as well.

Community

The snowboard community has grown into a global tribe. Without travelling to a foreign country, we can understand and relate to people from different cultures and faraway lands. The values, attitudes, and experiences establish a bond with people we might otherwise feel no connection to. As snowboarding becomes ingrained in our identity, we also join a communal support network including familiar faces and inspirational figures we may never meet. From the smallest accomplishments to the groundbreaking ones, your crew is there to share in them and help you along the way. We discover how fun and important it is to have others along for the ride in snowboarding and this concept applies throughout life.

85.

Powder Days

No friends on a powder day? More like everyone is a friend on a powder day. Seriously, chairlift rides are livelier, we hoot and holler at total strangers with complete understanding, and good will and good vibes are plentiful. Like holidays, they are catalysts to celebrating community.

86.

Support Network

Human nature inspires seeking support and membership within a community. It is natural and healthy, not a sign of weakness. Just think about how limiting it would be to always snowboard alone. Knowing that others have our backs is crucial in times of uncertainty or crisis, not to mention the advice, encouragement, inspiration, assistance, and the one half of high-fives that others provide. The way this plays out in snowboarding is worth your consideration whatever you do, wherever you are.

87.

Influence

The people, places, and activities that are prominent in your life will greatly influence who you become. The snowboard community values and promotes creativity, exploration, progression, acceptance, freedom, and happiness. In doing so, those characteristics are demonstrated in individuals. So choose your environment wisely for you will adapt to it mentally, emotionally, and physically.

88.

Share the Wealth

Happiness in anything is most deeply and truly felt when shared with others. It makes sense then that snowboarders consistently rate "good times with friends" as a top reason to ride as well as one of the greatest rewards of snowboarding. That is not to say you can't have a good time alone, you can and should. But make sure to maintain connections for sharing happiness whether it's with snowboarding or elsewhere.

Spirituality

The urge to interact with nature and sense that forces more powerful than us exist in the universe is how spirituality in snowboarding occurs for me. I have felt it on the best of days as well as the most challenging. It will no doubt mean different things to different people, but anyone who believes there is something intangible and deeply personal in snowboarding would likely include spirituality as part of the total package. What snowboarding demonstrates and often amplifies is that there are non-physical "things" that affect us and influence how we live our lives. To revere an experience or surroundings is to acknowledge the existence of something sacred. This is a real and necessary occurrence for the soul. If you can't find it riding, find it somewhere.

89.

Reverence

Every so often an experience while riding creates intense joy and awe that can be difficult to describe. Trying to capture and share it won't do it justice, similar to some attempts with photos. Maybe it's best to keep some moments private and develop a sense of reverence for universal mysteries, feeding the soul. That way you aren't tempted to alter an experience to meet someone else's outlook or perspective.

90.

Spirit and Soul

A person's spirit propels them forward in life. A strong spirit in snowboarding appears adventurous, open to possibilities, and accepting of challenges. Our souls on the other hand are more grounded in timeless qualities and elements of foundation. As such we refer to "soul riding" and people with soul as representative of the simpler aspects like a perfectly carved turn or genuine personalities. Snowboarding, as in life, is richer and more profound when spirit and soul are both honored and cultivated.

91.

Humility

Regardless of skill and experience, snowboarding can humble someone in an instant. As soon as invincibility sets in, the odds of a slam go up. A momentary loss of focus, freak terrain features, or another person suddenly appearing can send you rag-dolling without notice. We're all subject to randomness. You can choose your path, but expect the unexpected (and uncontrollable).

92.

Flow

Hard to define and personally unique, flow, or being in the zone, is an unmistakably deep and rewarding connection to an activity. So how do we get more of it? The recipe in snowboarding starts with total absorption in the present moment. With a dash of adrenaline, a pinch of danger, and a healthy portion of mindfulness we get a state of other-worldly, easy lightness and optimal performance. How you characterize it is up to you, but with awareness and development of our inner lives during physical activity we can experience more flow states in general.

Evolution

Our lives evolve in a manner similar to snow-boarding participation. The type of equipment or tools required will change according to circumstances. The people we rely on and interact with diversify with shifting interests. The locations that attract us transition along with our identity. There are also mental, physical, and spiritual developments occurring. Remember the way you were willing to adapt and evolve to fulfill snowboarding priorities whenever other priorities change.

93.

Compassion

When you watch a beginner struggle to stay up-right and positive do you

(a) Remember what that was like and offer support? or (b) Harass and heckle them to feel better about yourself? If it's (a) you are doing yourself and the flailing party a solid; a win-win. If (b) is more your style then it hurts you and them; a lose-lose. Compassion elevates both sides. This is so simple, but not necessarily an easy habit to develop. It might be easier to practice if you remember we all live and ride for happiness.

94.

Differences

Learning curves and challenges exist in urban, resort, and backcountry riding. This common ground is often forgotten in pettiness, insecurity, and negativity. Instead, focus on the impressive courage and talent. Your experience is the lens you can use to see how much skill and effort is involved in ALL types of riding. An inclusive perspective that is tolerant, even appreciative of differences, not only shows a higher level of intelligence and evolution but also feels much better than hating! If we can ride and let ride, we can live and let live.

95.

Priorities

Identifying and developing priorities is crucial to our individual evolution. Most winters begin with certain goals, wishes, ideas and such that we want to manifest. Then mid-season hits and if the snow isn't falling, momentum wanes, maybe to the point of negativity. Don't give up. Little things like tuning a board, exercising, and connecting with friends can still move us closer to our objectives and keep us ready to pounce on an opportunity. The point is to stay focused on priorities because situations can and will change quickly. One small thing per day can make a world of difference with priorities.

96.

Recreation is
Re-Creation

Despite the silly, playful nature of snowboarding, a tremendous amount of personal growth occurs that might not happen in a more serious context. The freedom from expectations, creative opportunities, and good ole rowdiness associated with snowboarding allow people enough space to grow as individuals. It also re-energizes us to handle more serious matters. Play, not relaxation, is the opposite of stress. The vitality from a day, season, or lifetime of riding is powerful medicine for mind, body, and spirit. Situations change, but our need for recreation does not.

Happiness

If there's one thing that all humans share it is the desire for happiness. There are a million ways to find it and the supply is unlimited. Although living for happiness may sound simple, we are very good at complicating, confusing, and forgetting what that means. Hopefully snowboarding can provide you a simplifying reminder and guidance toward genuine happiness and the skills to find it more often.

97.

Connect with your Environment

You make a choice to connect, via mind and board, with every place you ride. When place and priorities are in sync, the result is a physical and mental engagement that simplifies everything. This might be why snowboarding is fun wherever and however it goes down. Cultivate a meaningful connection in more environments and see what happens.

98.

Being Present

Being mentally present is a primary ingredient in the recipe for happiness. Snowboarding frees the mind from thoughts about the past or future by demanding your attention to the present moment. Dumping mental burdens creates the lightness you feel in a perfect, bottomless turn or soaring to a stomped landing. Reflect on these experiences and you can learn to intentionally engage in situations with a free and present mind.

99.

Keep it to Yourself

True happiness does not occur at anyone else's expense. Dissing, hating, or bringing misery to others is the result of insecurity and won't make you happy. It's crazy to see people spew negative energy at riders whose style or approach is different from their own. Get over it. Keep riding and living the way that makes you happy and forget about the rest.

100.

Mental Therapy

If you don't think snowboarding is therapeutic, notice how different you feel before and after a good session. As good as it feels it's not always easy. Snowboarding, like any therapeutic process, can be frustrating, challenging, and scary. But overcoming the obstacles, alone or with help, makes the effort worthwhile. Challenge yourself with honest introspection the way you do with snowboarding. The self-knowledge waiting to be discovered can also leave you stoked!

Author Bio

Nick Appl, snowboard addict since '96, holds college degrees in Outdoor Education and Psychology. His experience as a mental health professional includes residential, wilderness, and community-based rehabilitation programs serving adolescents and young adults. To support his snowboarding habit he's also been a construction laborer, waiter, lifty, breakfast cook, farm and ranch hand, commercial fisherman, landscaper, rental tech, RV skirting designer/installer, and with the publication of this book, an author. He lives in North Idaho with his wife, two daughters, two dogs and a cat.